A PICTORIAL HISTORY OF
FRANKLIN DELANO
ROOSEVELT

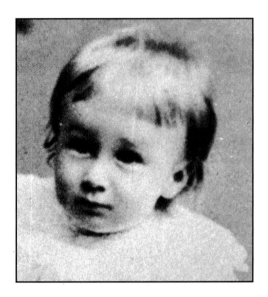

NIGEL BLUNDELL

Published in the USA 1996 by JG Press
Distributed by World Publications, Inc.

The JG Press is a trademark of
JG Press, Inc.
455 Somerset Avenue
North Dighton, MA 02764

This edition was produced in 1996 by the
Promotional Reprint Company Ltd

ISBN 1-57215-139-0

PICTURE ACKNOWLEDGMENTS
Every effort has been made to trace the ownership of all copyright material and to
secure permission from copyright holders. In the event of any question arising as to
the use of any material, we will be pleased to make the necessary corrections in
future editions.

The following pictures were supplied by the Hulton Deutsch Picture Library: 7, 15,
17, 19(b), 28, 33(l), 35(r), 36(tr).
The following pictures were held by the Imperial War Museum: 6, 18, 21, 62, 64.

Printed and bound in Hong Kong

CONTENTS

INTRODUCTION

THEY came from out of the fields and the factories, the small stores in the dusty towns and the Victorian homes where lemonade was sipped on sun-warmed porches. They came from cotton plantations and gas stations, from insurance offices and banks, from all walks of life to pay their respects to the great man in death. The train bearing the body of Franklin Delano Roosevelt trundled slowly through the Carolinas and Virginia, up through the Deep South, passing hundreds of thousands of men and women who stood as still as statues and who wept like babies.

The train bore the body of the 32nd president of the United States onwards to Washington where the flags flapped at half mast in the spring sunshine. He had died at his summer cottage, the Little White House, in Warm Springs, Georgia, on 12 April 1945. The following day the train came for his body and a nation that loved him like no other was plunged into deep and sincere mourning.

For FDR was a president like no other. Not only was he the architect of a social programme unparalleled in American history to rescue his suffering countrymen from the Great Depression, he was a democratic leader pitted against the worst threats to freedom ever to emerge in modern times – the nationalist expansionism of Nazi Germany and Imperial Japan. In his lifetime, he smashed the evil of the great poverty blighting his land and fuelled the 'arsenal of democracy' which vanquished the dictators. He had steered his nation through the rockiest and most perilous of times, dying with victory assured but still out of his sight.

For these achievements, his countrymen loved him – and for his loss they wept when he died. Eleanor Roosevelt, his widow travelling on that funeral cortège train, wrote: 'I was truly surprised by all the people

LEFT: A 1934 caricature emphasises the optimism that defined FDR's approach to life.

OPPOSITE: This official portrait, with its patriotic background, was made in wartime.

along the way. I didn't realise the full scope of the devotion to him until after he died.' Winston Churchill, Britain's wartime leader who forged an unbreakable personal bond with him, spoke for the free people of all lands when he told a hushed House of Commons upon receiving news of his death:

> In the days of peace he had broadened and stabilised the foundations of American life and union. In war he had raised the strength, might and glory of the great republic to a height never attained by any nation in history. But all this was no more than worldly power and grandeur, had it not been that the causes of human freedom and social justice, to which so much of his life had been given, added a lustre... which will long be discernible among men. For us it remains only to say that in Franklin Delano Roosevelt there died the greatest American friend we have ever known and the greatest champion of freedom who has ever brought help and comfort from the New World to the Old.

PRIVATE PAIN

THIS great architect of vision and victory (and also a man capable of intrigue and venality) was born into so much wealth that he could have idled his days happily in his native New York state, had he so wished, without ever entering the hurly-burly and uncertainty of public service. He came into a comforting world of social order and established riches on Monday, 30 January 1882, son of a wealthy investor and a socialite mother. His youth was spent being tutored by foreign teachers before, in 1896, he was old enough to attend Groton, the famous prep school. The young FDR – his middle name of Delano being his mother Sara's maiden name – excelled at sports and had a fair academic record, although he was by no means a child prodigy. His wife Eleanor would later say that in many respects he felt left out at school – a feeling which would later 'give him sympathy for all people who are left out.'

LEFT: Sara Delano Roosevelt, here with the young Franklin, was the daughter of a tea and opium trader, and descended from a family resident in Massachusetts since 1621.

OPPOSITE: The family of the proud father of Franklin, James Roosevelt, arrived in New Amsterdam (later New York) around 1650.

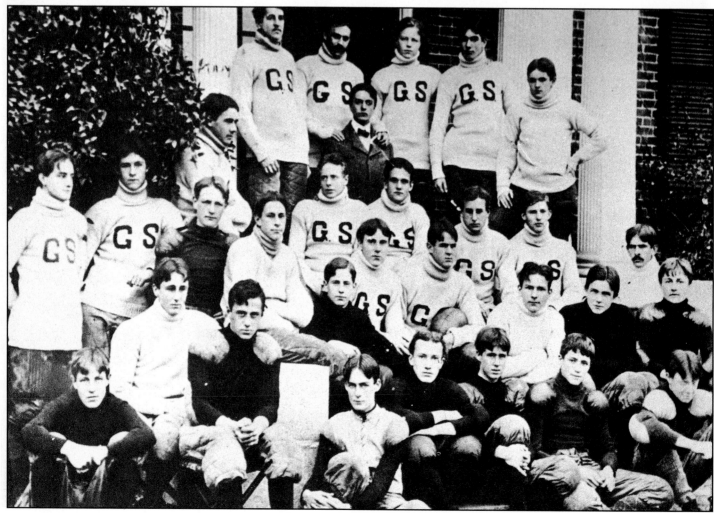

OPPOSITE TOP: Springwood, at Hyde Park on the Hudson River, was purchased in 1865 for $40,000 by Franklin's father James.

OPPOSITE BOTTOM: Franklin (front row, second from left) attended Groton School between 1896 and 1900, and played in the second eleven football squad.

RIGHT: At age 17, Franklin played an active part in the life of his school, and attained a position of some eminence. The drab brick buildings surrounding Harvard Yard now beckoned this scion of America's ruling class.

From Groton he went to Harvard University where, towards the end of his degree, he fell in love with his fifth cousin once removed, the 19-year-old Eleanor Roosevelt, whose uncle just happened to be Theodore Roosevelt, incumbent in the White House when they married in 1905. Franklin, married and soon to be a father, went from Harvard to another Ivy League institution, the law school at Columbia University. He passed his bar exam in 1907 and became a clerk at Carter, Ledyard and Milburn, a Wall Street law firm. In such a position, a man of his class and accomplishments could look forward to a lucrative career.

But FDR had a different vision. Even as a law clerk, he expressed a dream of running for public office, and even of one day being president. He described a path to the top, starting in the state legislature, and eventually being elected governor of New York. A run for the White House from the governor's mansion in Albany had been successfully accomplished by Grover Cleveland (1884) in Franklin's own lifetime, and cousin Theodore had been governor when he secured the Republicans' vice-presidential nomination in 1900. The assassination of President William McKinley in 1901 made Theodore president.

OPPOSITE: The Roosevelts summered at the family cottage on Campobello Island in the Bay of Fundy.

ABOVE: Franklin loved water sports, and in the summer of 1907 paddled this birch bark canoe at Campobello.

RIGHT: This was one of the last photographs taken of Franklin with his father James (right), who died during his son's freshman year at Harvard.

Where cousin Theodore's family, the Oyster Bay Roosevelts, had been Republicans since the time of Lincoln, Franklin's clan, the Hyde Park Roosevelts, had retained a traditional loyalty among the New York Dutch to the Democrats. However, in New York state the Democrats were inextricably entangled with the most notorious of the nation's political machines – Tammany Hall. Tammany ran New York city, and represented the huddled masses of immigrants who had fetched up in America's biggest port. Tammany candidates unashamedly bartered public services for votes, and their graft in office was, if beyond prosecution, well known. Franklin found Tammany noxious. He opted instead to seek nomination in upstate New York, where Democrats were seen more as quaint survivals of the old New York party founded by Aaron Burr and George and DeWitt Clinton in the days of George Washington and Thomas Jefferson. In 1910 he ran for the New York State Senate, and won.

LEFT: Cousin Theodore Roosevelt was president while Franklin was at Harvard. Teddy offered Franklin a model path for the ascent to the presidency.

OPPOSITE LEFT: In 1910 Franklin was elected to the New York State Senate.

OPPOSITE RIGHT: Woodrow Wilson won the Democratic nomination for president at the 1912 convention in part thanks to Franklin's efforts to promote his candidacy among the delegates. Franklin's reward was an appointment as assistant secretary of the Navy.

His first term in the State Senate was distinguished by his enthusiasm for conservation measures, or laws regulating hunting and fishing. Tammany, by contrast, began to promote measures that regulated the hours worked by women and children. Roosevelt tested the possibility of organising an anti-Tammany faction in New York's Democrats. As a result, he was pointedly excluded from the party's delegation to the presidential candidate's nominating convention that year. Roosevelt went anyway, at his own expense, to encourage uncommitted delegates to vote for the governor of New Jersey and eventual nominee, Woodrow Wilson. In the 1912 election Roosevelt was re-elected with a plurality of votes in his district; Tammany did not support him, although neither did it oppose him. Wilson also won, and the Democrats returned to the White House for the first time in 16 years. When Roosevelt went down to Washington, DC, for the inauguration on 4 March 1913, he was hoping to get a federally-appointed civil service post, such as customs collector for the port of New York. Instead, just like cousin Theodore in the 1890s, he received an offer to become assistant secretary of the Navy. He jumped at the offer, saying: 'All my life I have loved ships… and the assistant secretaryship is the one place, above all others, I would love to hold.'

Roosevelt's time as assistant secretary was dominated by the First World War (1914-18), which the United States entered in 1917. He was at the administrative heart of the US Navy's efforts. In 1918 he visited London and Paris, and made a tour of the Western Front. When he returned to Washington in October 1918, he went to Wilson to ask if he could be reassigned to active service – a request that was denied. Then the war ended in November.

With a solid reputation after seven years of public service, in 1920 he received the Democratic nomination for vice president, as running mate to James Cox of Ohio. The pair lost resoundingly to Warren Harding and Calvin Coolidge, which ushered in 12 years of Republican control of the White House. Roosevelt accepted his defeat with a good heart, being only 38, and set about making some serious money in private enterprise, becoming vice-president of a bond company. His plans were totally disrupted in 1921 when he suffered the affliction that divided his life in two.

LEFT: Eleanor Roosevelt, Franklin's cousin and Theodore Roosevelt's niece, reads to their large family.

OPPOSITE: Secretary of the Navy Josephus Daniels presents Franklin with a farewell gift on the latter's departure from office in 1920.

He went with his wife and his sons – he and Eleanor had six children, one of whom died in infancy – to Campobello, an island off the New Brunswick coast, where he came down with polio. He was never again able to regain muscular power below the waist, and for months it took all his strength simply to sit up straight in bed. Author Robert Leckie says of him in *Delivered from Evil, The Saga of World War Two*:

For all the pain and exhaustion and depression that his ordeal caused him, and the suffering it inflicted on his family, Franklin Roosevelt remained doggedly determined to pursue his political career. FDR would never walk again unassisted. Although he learned to handle canes and leg braces – 'my irons' as he called them – he still needed an attendant. To rise from a chair he had to seize the attendant's shoulder.

LEFT: Admiral William S Sims (right) was sent to London on Franklin's recommendation to act as liaison officer during the First World War.

OPPOSITE: Franklin in Rock Creek Park in April 1920 – a politician who was on the brink of national fame as the Democrats' vice-presidential nominee, and with the possibility of the White House in his future.

Roosevelt spent the next few years fighting for health, refusing to submit to his debilitating condition. He moved to Warm Springs, Georgia, where he swam in the thermal waters, building up powerful chest and arm muscles. Soon he was able to ride a horse, drive a specially modified car and, by 1928, could unsteadily rise with a cane and braces, but never without someone assisting him. In the same year, when such a condition would almost automatically rule out someone pursuing public life, he was persuaded by Democrat friends to run for the office of governor of New York – and won with a slim majority of 25,000 votes out of just over four million.

LEFT: Franklin stands with his 1920 running mate, the Democratic nominee for president, James M Cox of Ohio.

OPPOSITE: The hale and hearty Franklin Roosevelt at the age of 38 would be stricken within a year by poliomyelitis.

A New Deal

IN 1928 the cold winds of the Great Depression, which would be officially born the following year, were already beginning to blow. A lot of business was being done on credit, and trouble ensued when repayments could not be met. Farms were failing, as were their crops, and banks were starting to complain of grim times ahead. They were the portents of a storm of titanic dimensions which would change not just the United States but the world. For his part, Roosevelt's illness had increased his social conscience just at a time when the working person needed a friend in high places. He spoke in favour of state-run unemployment insurance, worked hard to regulate the price of electricity to the consumer and, in 1931, secured the creation of a new state agency that used public money for projects to alleviate unemployment.

Sometimes he was successful in getting what he wanted, sometimes not. But friend and foe alike recognised in him a genuine concern for his fellow man. He bartered and did dubious deals with political enemies, but justified it to his conscience by saying it was for the public good. His actions led *The Nation*, a left-wing political paper, to comment: 'His weakness and readiness to compromise have been evident – as have his personal charm and absolute integrity.'

That integrity would serve him until the end of his days. If he compromised or was weak, it made no difference to the good opinion of the New York electorate, who voted him in as governor for a second term in 1930 with the largest majority ever.

Left: FDR speaks during a whistlestop tour of the northern Great Plains states during the 1932 presidential election.

Opposite: Herbert Hoover addresses the nation at his inauguration in 1929. The moral poverty of his politics of self-reliance and private enterprise was revealed in its inability to alleviate economic hardship during the Depression.

LEFT: Panicking investors gather outside the Stock Exchange in New York during the Wall Street Crash of October 1929.

OPPOSITE LEFT: An unemployed man, a victim of the Depression, pleads for work on the streets of Detroit in 1931.

OPPOSITE RIGHT: This photograph, taken in 1930 when Roosevelt was governor of New York, shows his leg braces. Normally his disability was kept from public view.

Now Democrat bigwigs began mentioning his name as a potential candidate for the presidency. The press of the day protected his own frailties. Reporters never referred to his near-total paralysis below the waist, while photographers never took pictures of him seated in a wheelchair. He affected a long, flowing cloak which covered the chair he sat in and the useless limbs resting in it. But his mind and his energy were never affected by the polio. His was a magnetism that the Democratic leadership was determined to harness, physical limitations or not.

And just as the newspapers were happy to turn a blind eye to his disability, they were also willing to turn their attention away from something else they knew he needed to keep covered up – his love life. An unfaithful president would never survive without the connivance of a compliant press corps, and connive they did – never mentioning the long-running affair with his wife's social secretary, which clearly went to the very heart of his moral character.

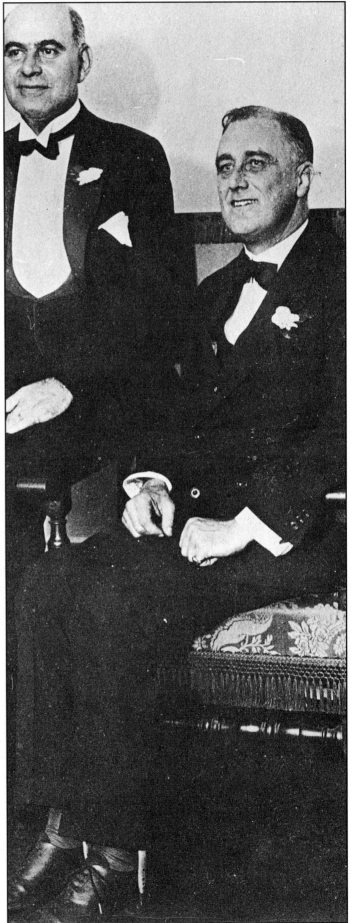

NOW YOU CAN HAVE A ROOSEVELT

in your white house at surprisingly low cost.

The Candidate with the Monitor top.

The Only Candidate with Campaign Control and Floating Power

Protected from either Dryness or Wetness . . . .
Silent—No Whirring Noises About Prohibition

A Roosevelt Campaign Manager Keeping His Ear to the Ground to Insure Voter Satisfaction

• A ROOSEVELT requires no attention . . . not even oiling. It is hermetically sealed against all opinions, thus insuring a smooth-running president.

KEEP REGULAR WITH ROOSEVELT

Roosevelt had fallen in love with blue-blooded Lucy Mercer while he was assistant secretary of the Navy, and the romance had been actively encouraged by some members of his family who preferred her to the strong-willed Eleanor. Alice Roosevelt, his wicked-tongued cousin, invited them both to dinner one night and waspishly defended her actions later to other clan members by saying: 'Franklin deserved a good time. He was married to Eleanor!'

It was while he was ill with influenza in 1918 that Eleanor discovered love letters from Lucy in his correspondence – deeply intimate letters that drove her to threaten him with divorce if he ever saw her again. Roosevelt, with his eyes on the main prize, broke off the affair. But it was resumed later, and indeed discovered later by those in the highest circles of the government and their newspaper contacts. His dalliance forever changed his relationship with his wife, who carved out her own niche in history as the strongest-willed First Lady of them all.

The judgment of history is that Roosevelt's tangled love life never interfered with his sense of duty to the nation. Peter Collier and David Horowitz, in their penetrating 1995 study of the duo entitled *The Roosevelts – An American Saga*, wrote: 'It was politics, not love and forgiveness, that helped them to learn to speak to each other again.'

Several things marked FDR down for leadership after his tour of duty in the naval post: experience at the local level, experience in Washington, good oratorical skills, good public image, an apparently supportive family and a clear vision of how the United States should be.

Four years' recuperation at Warm Springs, where he saw the rural poverty of the Deep South in all its grim reality, convinced him that social change had to be effected from Washington. The Great Depression had begun in 1929 with the collapse of the stock market, and the world was plunged headlong into a crisis that would prove a prelude to global war. Roosevelt decided that the time was ripe to run for president, and

OPPOSITE LEFT: An anti-Roosevelt leaflet issued during the 1932 election suggests he is a man of no political views.

OPPOSITE RIGHT: A demonstration for Roosevelt takes place at the 1932 Democratic convention.

ABOVE: Al Smith, the Democratic presidential candidate for 1928, was FDR's predecessor and political patron in New York state during the 1920s.

RIGHT: *The New York Times* reports Roosevelt's victory in the 1932 election.

on 22 January 1932 allowed his name to be put on the 15 March North Dakota Democratic primary ballot. Roosevelt gathered round him a coterie of journalists, professors and economists whom the press dubbed 'the Brain Trust', and on whom he relied to help transform his vision of America into reality. He also skilfully managed the nominating convention, and won on the fourth ballot.

With his party behind him, he barnstormed the United States, taking his message against the incumbent Republican Herbert Hoover to the furthest reaches of the Union. 'I stumped the country for no other reason than I wanted to get acquainted with the people,' he said.

Critics derided the lack of substance in many of his speeches, branding his policies 'platitudes and generalisations', but he was the right man at the right time. If nothing else, he promised the repeal of Prohibition, the anti-alcohol law which made life miserable for many but made fortunes for mobsters like Al Capone. More importantly, under Hoover the economy of his country was in danger of succumbing to the Depression. Banks were failing, a dispossessed army of men crossed the land on railcars looking for work, the farmers of the Midwest faced ruin and repossession of their mortgaged property and the docks were idle. Many who lived through this time believed the United States stood at the brink of the kind of revolution that had wracked Imperial Russia at the end of the First World War.

LEFT: FDR's running mate in the 1932 election was John Nance Garner (right), the Speaker of the House. Garner was from Texas, and harboured presidential ambitions of his own, which burst into the open during the 1940 election when FDR ran for a third term. His treachery earned him replacement by Henry Wallace of Iowa, who himself ran for president in 1948.

RIGHT: Joseph Zangara (centre), an Italian bricklayer, fired five shots at FDR on 15 February 1932 in Miami, Florida. Chicago Mayor Anton Cermak was hit instead, and died in March. Zangara went to the electric chair.

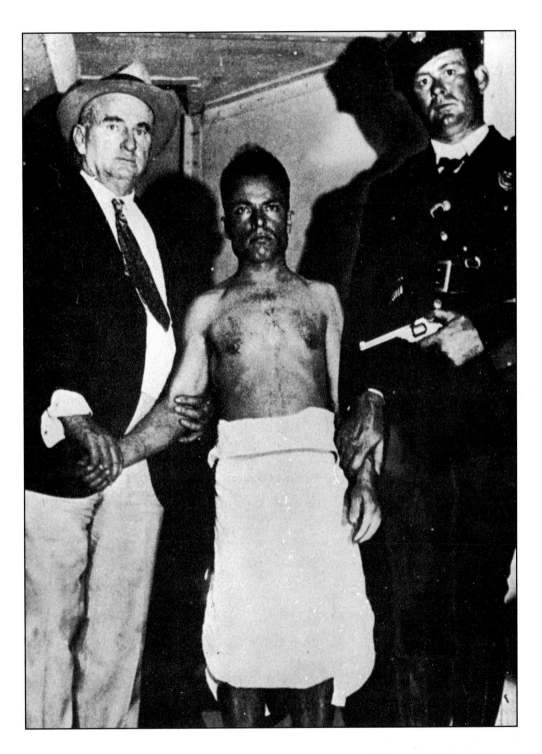

But revolution did not come. Instead, in November of that year, those who voted for Franklin Delano Roosevelt swept the do-nothing Republicanism of Herbert Hoover away. And FDR swore to change things. In the speech he gave at his inauguration as the 32nd president the following March, he spoke with words of hope; words in peacetime that would rival those of Winston Churchill's across the Atlantic in wartime. Sensing the fright seizing the country by the throat, he told his countrymen:

Let me assert my firm belief that the only thing we have to fear is fear itself – nameless, unreasoning, unjustified terror which paralyses needed efforts to convert retreat into advance. In every dark hour of our national life, a leadership of frankness and vigour has met with that understanding and support of the people themselves which is essential to victory. I am convinced that you will again give that support to leadership in these critical days.

LEFT: This song was written to celebrate the hope given to the nation by one of FDR's New Deal agencies, the National Recovery Administration.

OPPOSITE: The blue eagle of the NRA became a familiar sight in 1930s America. Careful viewers will even spot it amid the credits of Hollywood films.

Compared with the perils that our forefathers conquered because they believed and were not afraid, we have still much to be thankful for. Nature still offers her bounty and human efforts have multiplied it.

Plenty is at our doorstep, but a generous use of it languishes in the very sight of the supply. Primarily this is because the rulers of the exchange of mankind's goods have failed, through their own stubbornness and their own incompetence, have admitted their failure, and abdicated. The moneychangers have fled from their high seats in the temple of our civilisation. We may now restore that temple to the ancient truths.

Telling them that he was going to introduce an unprecedented programme of emergency relief works, he went on: 'The nation asks for action and action now! We must act and act quickly.'

In the first, now famous, 100 days between March and June 1933 his administration rushed through measure after measure aimed at reviving the comatose patient that was the United States of America. Finance and banking were regulated by new laws that loosened credit and insured the saver's deposits.

He brought the US off the gold standard and instituted four major bodies to bring about a nationwide recovery: the Civilian Conservation Corps, the National Recovery Administration, the Agricultural Adjustment Administration and the Public Works Administration. His aims were twofold: to revive American industry and to jump-start the economy with the biggest programme of public works seen in the nation's history. The National Emergency Council was also formed to oversee all efforts and ensure maximum efficiency.

His programme of regeneration was christened the New Deal, from a line in his acceptance speech at the nominating convention. While this compact between a government and its people had its detractors, notably among the rich and among some union leaders, it was a deal that delivered. The mammoth Hoover Dam in Nevada was completed under it. The Gulf of Mexico was linked with the Great Lakes via the Illinois Waterway. Other major projects were in the areas of forestry, road building, petroleum and municipal building. There was also legislation that gave trade unions the right to organise and bargain collectively.

OPPOSITE: FDR signs a New Deal measure, the Farm Credit Act, into law in June 1933.

ABOVE: Watts Bar Dam on the Tennessee River was one of the dams of the Tennessee Valley Authority (TVA). Former president Jimmy Carter recalled for American television in 1982 the first time he saw a light bulb switched on in his home – using electricity from the hydroelectric power projects of the TVA.

RIGHT: A map shows the layout of the TVA, whose projects brought government money to five states.

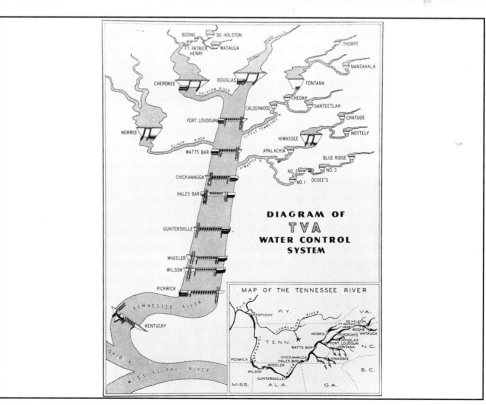

LEFT: The Works Progress Administration (WPA) used public money to put people to work on small public projects. Its small offices dotted the country.

President Roosevelt realised, like Adolf Hitler in Germany, the importance of the radio as a medium to get a message across. He began a new policy of speaking directly to the American people in 'fireside chats', most of which he used in the early days to spell out the reasons for his dramatic measures. For it soon became clear that Roosevelt was not just intent on economic recovery, but of wide-reaching social plans intended to change the face of the United States forever. These plans that included bringing electrification to rural areas, to protect the income of farmers where no protection existed before and to give the 'little man' a sense that, finally, someone cared. Under Hoover's administration, handouts were loans that had to be repaid by workers living on the poverty line. Roosevelt changed all that.

It was by no means Utopia, however, and not everyone – including some of his own advisers – shared his vision. Quarrels within his own camp became a regular feature of his first administration. One of his administrators called his programmes 'a movement towards slavery, towards a type of Chamber of Commerce Guild Fascism.'

RIGHT: A member of the United Cannery, Agricultural, Packing and Allied Workers of America proudly displays his union membership book. New Deal legislation guaranteed the American worker the right to join a trade union.

RIGHT: The Dust Bowl was a natural disaster that struck the Plains states during the 1930s as huge clouds of dust caused by a combination of drought and soil erosion settled on once-fertile farmland. The New Deal encouraged conservation measures that helped to prevent such disasters.

ABOVE: FDR speaks to the citizens of Bismarck, North Dakota, in 1936.

LEFT: Eleanor looks on as FDR receives a warm welcome in Worcester, Massachusetts, during the 1936 election.

OPPOSITE TOP: When FDR defeated Republican Alf Landon in November 1936, he achieved the highest total of electoral votes then recorded, 523.

OPPOSITE BELOW LEFT: A *Punch* cartoon satirises FDR's plan to appoint six more justices.

OPPOSITE BELOW RIGHT: The Wagner Act gave unions, such as the United Auto Workers, the legal backing to organise under the most anti-labour of employers.

ROOSEVELT SWEEPS THE NATION; HIS ELECTORAL VOTE EXCEEDS 500; LEHMAN WINS; CHARTER ADOPTED

FEW HOUSE SHIFTS

Democrats May Add to Vast Majorities in Both Chambers

THREE SENATORS TRAIL

Barbour, Hastings and Metcalf Appear to Have Lost Seats.

90 HOUSE RACES IN DOUBT

Democrats Elect 254, While Republicans Obtain 84, and Progressives 6.

By TURNER CATLEDGE

Republican hopes of making heavy inroads upon the huge Democratic majorities in Congress were apparently smothered under the pro-Roosevelt landslide in yesterday's election.

As the size of the New Deal avalanche continued to grow into the

Landon Congratulates President, Who Replies

Special to The New York Times.
TOPEKA, Wednesday, Nov. 4.—Governor Landon conceded his defeat in a message of congratulation to President Roosevelt at 1:30 o'clock this morning, Eastern standard time.

His message read as follows:
"The nation has spoken. Every American will accept the verdict and work for the common cause of the good of our country. That is the spirit of democracy. You have my sincere congratulations."

"ALF M. LANDON."

Governor Landon decided to send the message after he had retired for the night at the Executive Mansion, with the word that no statement would be issued during the night.

Special to The New York Times.
HYDE PARK, N. Y., Wednesday, Nov. 4.—Half an hour after receiving Governor Landon's message President Roosevelt sent the following reply:

"I am grateful to you for your generous telegram and I am confident that all of us Americans will now pull together for the common good. I send you every good wish."

UNION PARTY VOTE FAR BELOW BOASTS

Coughlin Group Appears to

BIG CHARTER VOTE

8-Hour System for Firemen Also Wins Easily

VOTING CHANGE APPROVED

Brunner Is Victor Over Morris by Large Plurality.

ROOSEVELT SWEEP HERE

President's Vote and Margin, Which Reached 1,356,458, Set Highest City Record.

By RUSSELL B. PORTER

President Roosevelt piled up the largest vote and plurality ever accorded to a candidate for any office in the history of New York City at yesterday's election.

With all the city's 3,796 election districts in, the President had the extraordinary plurality of 1,356,458

Smith Plans Comment On the Election Today

Alfred E. Smith, former Democratic candidate for President who espoused the cause of Alfred M. Landon in this campaign said last night that he probably would issue a statement today setting forth his views on President Roosevelt's sweeping victory.

Earlier in the evening he had called The New York Times to ask how the election was going. He was informed that President Roosevelt was leading in all but a handful of States. He made no comment but when he was asked if he were going to a party of Jeffersonian Democrats in the apartment of Raoul Desvernine, Liberty League lawyer, to which he had been invited, he replied: "No, I'm going to bed."

P. S.—The former Governor did not retire at once. He called up an hour later to get the latest returns.

DEMOCRATS RETAIN STATE SENATE LEAD

They Are Assured of 30 Seats of the 51, One More Than Their Previous Number.

FAIL TO WIN ASSEMBLY

LEHMAN VOTE CUT

Bleakley Gets a Surprising Total in the City

SWEEP HELPS GOVERNOR

Roosevelt Strong in Industrial Cities—Gets Big Up-State Poll.

OTHER DEMOCRATS SAFE

Bray, Tremaine, Bennett and Others of State Ticket Regarded Certain of Victory.

By JAMES A. HAGERTY

Governor Herbert H. Lehman was re-elected Governor of New York yesterday for a third term. The indicated plurality for the Governor over former Supreme Court Justice William F. Bleakley, his Republican opponent, was about 600,000.

Governor Lehman, who was urged

POLL SETS RECORD

Roosevelt Electoral Vote of 519 Seen as a Minimum

NO SWING TO THE BOLTERS

'Jefferson Democrats' Fail to Cause Rift as Expected.

NEIGHBORS HAIL PRESIDENT

Landon Concedes Defeat and Sends His Congratulations to Victorious Rival.

By ARTHUR KROCK

Accepting the President as the issue, nearly eight million more voters than ever before had gone to the polls in the United States—about 45,000,000 persons—yesterday gave to Franklin Delano Roosevelt the most overwhelming testimonial

LEFT: Henry Ford's thugs beat up a United Auto Workers' organiser for merely handing out leaflets. The bitterness of American labour's struggles for union recognition is often forgotten nowadays, yet would be very familiar to those active in organising unions in Third World countries today.

Of his critics, Roosevelt later wrote: 'They were unable to realise that permanent recovery was impossible without the eradication of the economic and social maladjustments which permitted wealth and prosperity to concentrate in the control of a few.'

By the new year, 1934, many conservative factions in the United States supported the New Deal. His measures had increased employment, improved labour conditions, stemmed the tide of business failures and inspired hope. But other reactionaries and conservatives branded Roosevelt a Bolshevik. The rich attacked the new taxes they were forced to pay, while some of the poor were unhappy with the level of relief they received. The courts overturned some of his reforms as unconstitutional, while trading partners abroad complained of unfair tariffs. Yet taken overall, most Americans were heartened by the measures. Roosevelt told his critics that he was not a revolutionary. He was later to explain: 'The task of reconstruction did not

RIGHT: Louisiana's Governor Huey Long transformed his state into a personal fief by using the powers of patronage vested in his office. His own presidential ambitions set him against FDR, and his plans for a guaranteed income for every American family threatened the heart of the New Deal coalition.

BELOW: John L Lewis, president of the United Mine Workers from 1920 to 1960, founded the Congress of Industrial Organisations to establish collective bargaining in industries such as the steel and automobile ones during the 1930s. This step gave labour a greater presence in the American political landscape.

LEFT: FDR's jaunty public face conveys the affable persona he used – to devastating effect – to manipulate his allies and enemies.

OPPOSITE: A cartoon comment on FDR's fireside chats – one of his granddaughters complains about his speech running over into Ed Wynn's show.

call for the creation of strange values. It was rather finding the way again to old, but somewhat forgotten ideals and values.'

Criticism and carping remained throughout his first administration, but by the time he came to fight the second election in 1936 *The Economist* said: 'Mr Roosevelt may have given the wrong answers to many of his problems. But he is at least the first president of modern America who has asked the right questions.'

Roosevelt was returned to office in November of 1936 after a bitterly fought campaign, winning a landslide victory in which he carried every state of the union except for Maine and Vermont. Yet while victory tasted sweet, grave problems confronted him – not just at home, where the ravages of the Depression had still not been eradicated, but overseas. The spectre of rising German militarism and Japanese aggression was beginning to show. They were forces which would test President Roosevelt's mettle to the limit.

Conservative opponents in the United States criticised Roosevelt as 'that man in the White House'; the pace of his reforms had slowed, but their anger against him increased. Roosevelt, frustrated by the decision of the Supreme Court to overturn some of his New Deal measures during his first administration, tried to stack the court with judges favourable to him, a move that both opponents and supporters saw as dangerously close to the act of a would-be dictator. Indeed, Roosevelt, relying on his mammoth majority

LEFT: Listening to one of FDR's 'fireside chats'.

OPPOSITE: Father Charles E Coughlin, a radical Catholic priest, who at first admired and then attacked Roosevelt's policies.

and cosy image among the electorate, actually set forth on his planned reshuffle without consulting party leaders. It was a dangerous ploy and one that was ultimately unsuccessful.

The president blamed the court for laying 'a dead hand' on much of his legislation, claiming that it had not allowed the federal government to function 'as people had voted for it to function'. The row which ensued over his attempts to restructure the court, so that it would be more in his favour, was the first serious political defeat he suffered. Yet in the end, through retirement, ill health and death, he largely achieved his aims, managing to place many of the liberals he wanted. Political commentator Alan Jackson said: 'He tried to get them in the back door and got found out. In the end they walked in the front door anyway. It was a sign of his impetuosity and an almost God-like belief in the righteousness of what he had embarked on for his country that he tried it in the first place.'

That there had been an easing of suffering for 13 million unemployed Americans was undeniable. But the dragon of depression, while wounded, had not yet been slaughtered. In a temporary reversal of his major public works programme, and in order to revive the business economy further, Roosevelt ordered a cutback in government spending. But it only served to cause further recession. Business indexes dropped from 110 to 85, unemployment surged again and steel operations in the giant mills of Pittsburgh and Cleveland were down to 30 per cent of capacity. The political weekly *New Republic*, usually so loyal to FDR, lamented to its readers 'the wreckage of Mr Roosevelt's second term'. Yet his contract with America, in the shape of the New Deal, went on; its popularity among the hard-pressed working classes never wavered. It had set out to secure for American labour the right to bargain collectively, the regulation of hours and wages and the public provision of a pension through Social Security – all were accomplished by 4 July 1938.

ABOVE: FDR with friend and advisor Louis Howe.

ELEANOR

'After all, Eleanor Roosevelt was a last (the last? the only?) flower of that thorny Puritan American conscience which was, when it was good, very, very good, and now it's quite gone things are horrid.' So wrote the masterful American writer, Gore Vidal, in an essay in 1971. It was a fair judgment on the first First Lady.

Eleanor Roosevelt had a difficult personal life for which an absorbing public career may have offered some compensation. Her father, Elliott Roosevelt, the brother of Theodore the president, was an alcoholic. This addiction kept him out of Eleanor's life, although he loved her deeply.

Eleanor's mother, Anna Hall Roosevelt, regarded her eldest daughter as almost ugly, and in that sense a disappointment to a woman whose own face had been thought a handsome one when she debuted in society. She made her preference for the company of Eleanor's brothers clear.

In 1892 Elliott's drinking and womanising proved too much for Anna, who set up a separate household. She began to treat Eleanor more

BELOW: Franklin and Eleanor chat on a porch in the summer of 1904. They were already secretly engaged.

affectionately in these changed circumstances. But in November Anna contracted diphtheria; in December she died. In her will, she requested that her mother be made her children's guardian. This act proved full of foresight – Elliott died after a fall in August 1894 when Eleanor was 9.

Eleanor withdrew into herself. But this sad solitude was to change, thanks to the plans for her education laid down by her mother. In 1899 she was sent to Allenswood, a finishing school in the London suburbs run by a Frenchwoman, Mlle Souvestre. There she was popular with the other girls, and in Mlle Souvestre she for the first time found a parental figure who was not absent or indifferent.

At the end of this happy time she returned to the United States in 1902. Her coming out in New York society was more welcome among older men who enjoyed intelligent conversation than young ones looking for a wife. But that summer she had met her cousin Franklin on a train, and they began a tentative courtship once the social season got underway in the autumn. They married after a lengthy secret engagement in March 1905. Eleanor became pregnant on honeymoon, and gave birth to a daughter in 1906. It was the first of five children, and the only girl.

As Franklin started his political career, Eleanor took up the role of the supportive wife. While she focused on her duties as a wife and mother, Eleanor was also watching the way things worked in the nation's capital.

The shock of her life came when she discovered Franklin's letters from Lucy Mercer when he was ill with double pneumonia in the autumn of 1918. The two were having an affair, which apparently had been going on for some time. Since Lucy Mercer was an attractive woman with a fun-loving personality – so unlike the earnest, plain Eleanor – it was an especially bitter blow. She served Franklin an ultimatum – divorce her or break off his relations with Lucy Mercer. A divorce would almost certainly have destroyed Franklin's political career, so he and Eleanor took a trip to Europe on government business to effect a reconciliation.

When Franklin ran as vice-presidential candidate in the 1920 election, Eleanor accompanied him on a campaign trip. So after Franklin was stricken with polio in 1921, the role of his stand-in was not entirely alien to her. She would attend meetings of political committees, keep in touch with the political gossip and developed views of her own, which she was able to act on following her husband's election to the presidency.

Her radical attitude to the role of the First Lady was demonstrated on 6 March 1933 when, two days before the president, she gave her first press conference – something no First Lady had done before. Eleanor attained a high media profile, writing a syndicated column and going on the lecture circuit. As a result of her expressing opinions that struck many as verging on socialism, she became a figure Republicans hated.

She used her influence when Franklin was in office to promote the cause of women's rights in the face of the fierce spoils system of American politics: she would do all she could to protect talented Republican woman from being replaced by Democratic men. She also did all she could to increase opportunities for African-Americans, which in the colour-bar climate of the time was not very much.

In 1920, Franklin's campaign team had included a young and lively woman named Marguerite Le Hand, whom he'd hired as his secretary following the Democrats' defeat. Although there was no hard evidence of an affair between the two, the level of intimacy they attained was widely acknowledged by those who saw it to be comparable to that of a husband and wife. Eleanor acquiesced in this relationship, whatever its dimensions.

During the war she travelled widely, wherever American men and women were serving. Afterwards she was active in the United Nations, serving as chairman of the Commission on Human Rights (1946-51) and as a US representative to the UN General Assembly (1946-52).

She also remained a Democratic political activist, enthusiastically supporting Adlai Stevenson for president in the 1952 and 1956 elections, and opposing the nomination of John F Kennedy in the 1960 one. She died in 1962, and four presidents – past and future – attended her funeral.

ABOVE: The Roosevelts in July 1932. Standing at the back from the left are Elliott, James, John and Franklin Jr. Seated at the front are Franklin Sr, Eleanor with granddaughter Sisty, Anna with son Curtis Jr, and Franklin Sr's mother Sara.

CLOUDS OF WAR

THE twin demons of poverty and unemployment were, by the end of the 1930s, now easily being overshadowed by the clouds of war gathering across much of the world. Roosevelt, like most presidents before him, had pursued a foreign policy of 'hands-off Europe'. He was outward-looking; he drew his country closer to Latin American nations under his Good Neighbour policy, treating them more equally. But he wanted no part in a foreign war which would kill thousands, if not hundreds of thousands, of American boys.

America's lesson in the First World War had been painful enough: almost 130,000 deaths after entering the war in its closing stages. Woodrow Wilson, the man whom Roosevelt had campaigned for, had been unable to lead his people into the League of Nations – doomed forerunner to the modern United Nations – and the United States had embraced the kind of 'splendid isolation' that had been the hallmark of imperial Britain at the end of the 19th century.

Roosevelt, unlike the statesmen of some European nations, had never let his guard slip in terms of national defence. His enthusiasm for the Navy ensured that America's armed forces were strong – and strongly funded – right up to the outbreak of the Second World War, although they were not a match for

LEFT: FDR and Eleanor attend naval manoeuvres in 1934 aboard the cruiser USS *Indianapolis*.

OPPOSITE: The feisty New York Mayor Fiorello La Guardia supported the New Deal.

the highly-prepared ranks of Germany and Japan. But even in 1936 the defence budget was a mammoth $1200 million.

In 1935 the president and his advisers had drawn up the Neutrality Act, giving him power to declare an embargo on shipments of arms, but not raw materials, to belligerents, and to warn US citizens that travel on belligerents' ships would be at their own risk. But Roosevelt, always hungry to stoke the dormant furnaces of idle American industry, proved himself inconsistent when it came to applying the act.

For instance, he went beyond the terms of the act in 1935 to discourage the shipment of raw materials to Italy during its Ethiopian adventure, but refused to stop war supplies to Japan in 1937 when she launched her bloody and brutal war against China. And FDR would not supply arms to the left-wing Spanish government that was fighting Franco's military rebellion.

Historians usually share the belief that FDR was muddled in his prewar foreign policy. He spoke in 1937 of 'quarantine' against international aggressors, but with little substance about how such policies might be effected. At a speech in Chicago that year, he said: 'It seems unfortunately true that the epidemic of world lawlessness is spreading. When an epidemic of physical disease starts to spread, the community joins in a quarantine of the patients in order to protect the health of the community against the spread of the disease.'

His call fell on deaf ears. The so-called victorious nations of the First World War – Britain and France – had bled themselves white in four years of trench warfare unparalleled in history; they had no stomach for quarantining Hitler's rising Germany. James Chace and Caleb Carr, authors of *America Invulnerable*, said of Roosevelt's efforts:

At the time of the Quarantine Speech he was trying to urge the nations of the world to find new ways of controlling aggression and at the same time to get a reading of American public opinion on the subject.

ABOVE: The popularity of FDR among the American people was due in part to his approachability.

OPPOSITE: A royal visit to Washington by King George VI took place in June 1939.

RIGHT: Albert Einstein's letter to FDR in October 1939 warning of German efforts to develop an atom bomb set in train the events that led to the United States becoming a nuclear superpower.

LEFT: Mussolini's ventures in Ethiopia in 1935-36 first alerted FDR to the dangers posed by the nationalists of the Axis powers to the long-term interests of the United States.

OPPOSITE: FDR at no time had any sympathy for the Nazi leader Adolf Hitler. He regarded the Nazi regime as a barbaric menace to civilisation, and was eager to do anything he could to quarantine it and ultimately overthrow it.

It was that reading, when it came, that caused him to back away from forceful action. Though many American citizens shared Roosevelt's shock at the behaviour of Japan, Germany and Italy and liked the overall tone of his speech, few were ready to support programmes that might lead to war. Roosevelt would later remark of this period: 'It is a terrible thing to look over your shoulder when you are trying to lead – and to find no one there.'

It was a vacillating policy at best. Time and again he promised the mothers of the United States that none of their sons would die in a foreign war. Yet alone in the White House Oval Office at night, chain smoking cigarettes and nursing a glass of bourbon, he could see war coming at full tilt. He abhorred the racist harangues of Hitler, and Japanese plans for a 'co-prosperity sphere of influence in South-East Asia'. Yet while continuing to steer a completely neutral course for the United States, he nevertheless drew closer to those nations he sensed would one day be pitted against the dictators in the showdown which would shape the world for years to come.

In 1938, after the state-sponsored anti-Jewish pogrom in Germany of *Kristallnacht*, Roosevelt recalled the American ambassador to Berlin. The same year, he granted sizable loans to China, which was engaged in a fierce war with Japan. The following year, he cemented relations with Britain still further with a reception of Britain's King George VI and Queen Elizabeth in Washington.

War came to Europe on 1 September 1939 when the German army stormed across Poland's borders, and civilians and soldiers alike were bombed by the German Air Force. Two days later, on a Sunday, the war became global when Britain, possessor of a mighty empire, announced that she was at war with Germany.

In the United States, President Roosevelt knew which side he was on, but his nation stayed neutral while its stockpiles of armaments grew increasingly high. In the run-up to war, he had increased the defence

expenditure budget by 10 per cent and wrung from Congress a further $800 million in funds for air defence programmes. The Supreme Court, which now had many of his hand-picked liberal justices on it, had banned sit-down strikes, which had been a regular occurrence during the previous year, and the factories were churning out armaments at an astonishing rate. Ultimately, and ironically, the Second World War would provide the United States with the best cure of all to the Great Depression.

Shortly before the outbreak of war, Roosevelt took a decision that would not only change the future of warfare, but of the world itself. One month before Hitler's tanks rolled, a German physicist named Albert Einstein, forced into exile because of his Jewish faith, wrote a memorandum to the president stating that atomic fission could be used to make bombs of incredible power. Einstein was asked to warn the president that two German physicists working under the Nazis had achieved the fission of uranium in experiments – and that the consequence of Hitler holding these terrible weapons was incalculable.

Taking heed of the memo, Roosevelt gave the authority for a small band of scientists, using land that once belonged to a Boy Scout troop in the small New Mexico town of Los Alamos, to undertake the mammoth research necessary to give the United States 'the bomb'. His sanction of the Manhattan Project, as it was codenamed, would later turn America from world power to superpower.

LEFT: Japanese artillery bombards Chinese positions during the Sino-Japanese War (1937-45). US-Japanese relations had always been difficult, and the rise to power of the militarists with their expansionary plans in Japan exacerbated this.

OPPOSITE: Troops of Franco's army crossed from Spanish North Africa to seize power from the constitutionally-elected left-wing government. American policy was strictly neutral in the ensuing civil war, and FDR failed to perceive how Hitler and Mussolini were using this war to further their own schemes.

THE NEUTRAL ALLY

ON 5 September 1939 Roosevelt broadcast to his people, declaring the United States would remain neutral towards the combatants in the war raging in the Old World. Yet he said the American people knew right from wrong, adding that the sympathies of America were with those nations fighting the Nazi menace. On 8 September, in order to keep all options open, Roosevelt ordered a limited state of emergency, which put all armed forces on an alert and warned shipping lines that their vessels were subject to seizure by the state for wartime use at a moment's notice.

On 7 October, Roosevelt again tried to maintain American isolationism, with his Declaration of Panama which banned belligerent naval activity within a 300-mile security zone off the coast of the Americas south of Canada. The following month, Congress, in a special session called by Roosevelt, repealed arms-embargo clauses of the 1937 Neutrality Act and began supplying the goods to Britain that would become her lifeline during the darkest years of the Second World War. Technically, the 'cash and carry' plan, as it was called, allowed any belligerent nation – Italy and Germany included – to sail its ships to American ports, load up with weapons, and sail away. In reality, the plan only helped Britain who, with her mighty battle and merchant fleets, was able to take advantage of this armaments lifeline.

LEFT: FDR had always been associated with the Eastern Establishment's Atlanticist politics of intervening in European affairs. Once war broke out in 1939, he had to tread carefully to avoid alienating the majority of Americans, who at that time wanted no involvement in Europe's business.

OPPOSITE: At the 1940 Democratic convention, FDR was nominated for an unprecedented third term.

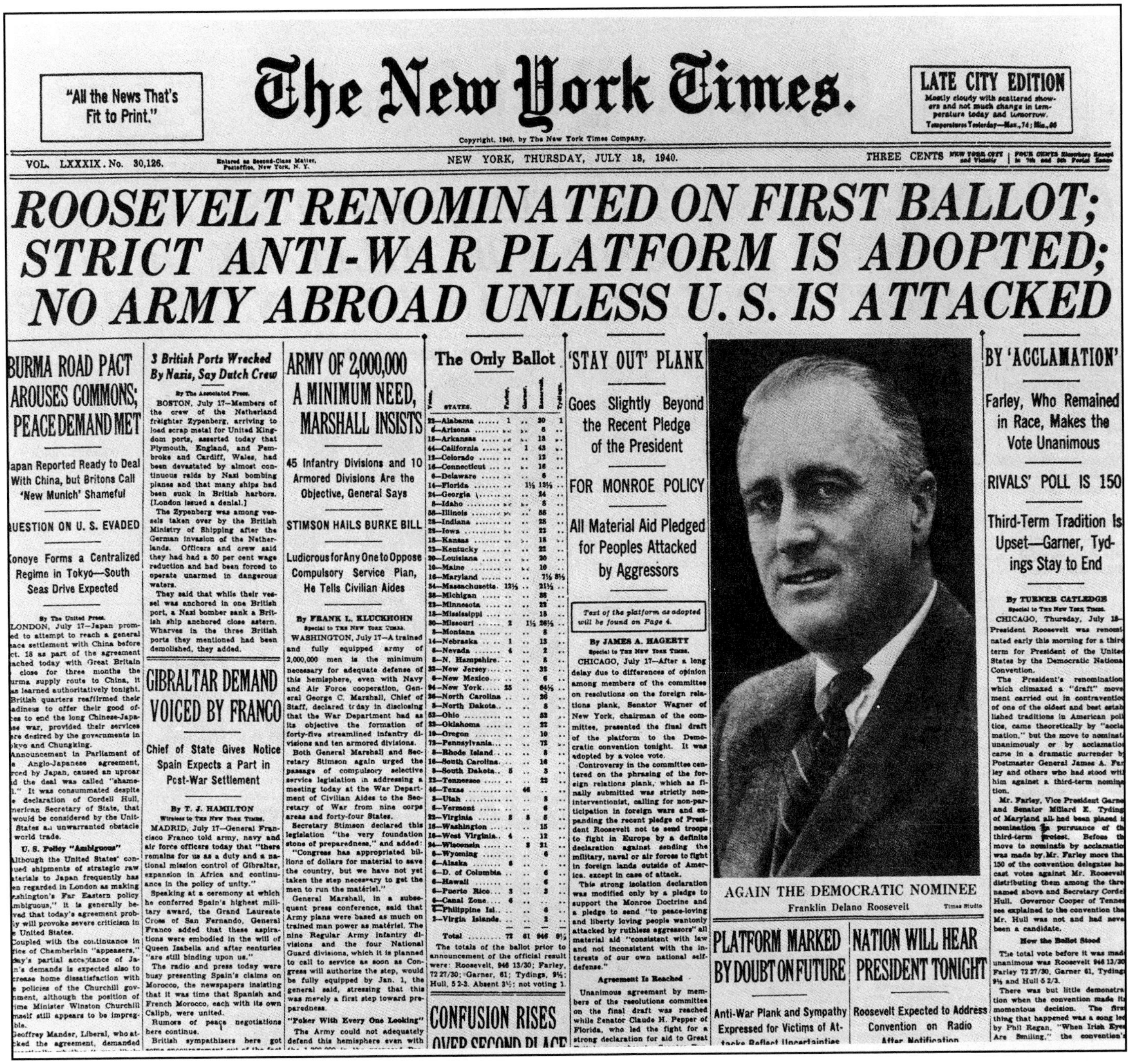

"All the News That's Fit to Print."

The New York Times.

LATE CITY EDITION
Mostly cloudy with scattered showers and not much change in temperature today and tomorrow.

Copyright, 1940, by The New York Times Company.

VOL. LXXXIX. No. 30,126. NEW YORK, THURSDAY, JULY 18, 1940. THREE CENTS

ROOSEVELT RENOMINATED ON FIRST BALLOT; STRICT ANTI-WAR PLATFORM IS ADOPTED; NO ARMY ABROAD UNLESS U. S. IS ATTACKED

BURMA ROAD PACT AROUSES COMMONS; PEACE DEMAND MET

Japan Reported Ready to Deal With China, but Britons Call 'New Munich' Shameful

QUESTION ON U. S. EVADED

Konoye Forms a Centralized Regime in Tokyo—South Seas Drive Expected

3 British Ports Wrecked By Nazis, Say Dutch Crew

GIBRALTAR DEMAND VOICED BY FRANCO

Chief of State Gives Notice Spain Expects a Part in Post-War Settlement

ARMY OF 2,000,000 A MINIMUM NEED, MARSHALL INSISTS

45 Infantry Divisions and 10 Armored Divisions Are the Objective, General Says

STIMSON HAILS BURKE BILL

Ludicrous for Any One to Oppose Compulsory Service Plan, He Tells Civilian Aides

By FRANK L. KLUCKHOHN

The Only Ballot

CONFUSION RISES OVER SECOND PLACE

'STAY OUT' PLANK

Goes Slightly Beyond the Recent Pledge of the President

FOR MONROE POLICY

All Material Aid Pledged for Peoples Attacked by Aggressors

Text of the platform as adopted will be found on Page 4.

By JAMES A. HAGERTY

AGAIN THE DEMOCRATIC NOMINEE
Franklin Delano Roosevelt

PLATFORM MARKED BY DOUBT ON FUTURE

Anti-War Plank and Sympathy Expressed for Victims of Attacks Reflect Uncertainties

NATION WILL HEAR PRESIDENT TONIGHT

Roosevelt Expected to Address Convention on Radio After Notification

BY 'ACCLAMATION'

Farley, Who Remained in Race, Makes the Vote Unanimous

RIVALS' POLL IS 150

Third-Term Tradition Is Upset—Garner, Tydings Stay to End

By TURNER CATLEDGE

Now the 'arsenal of democracy' was beginning to operate at full pitch, but Roosevelt still had no intention of pitching American youth into the maelstrom. In June 1940, however, when the Nazi armies turned on France and the Low Countries of Belgium and Holland, Roosevelt signalled to Americans that intervention could not be far away. In an ominous speech at the University of Virginia on the day that Germany invaded France, he said:

> On this tenth day of June 1940, the hand that held the dagger has struck it into the back of its neighbour. On this tenth day of June 1940, in this university, founded by the first great teacher of American democracy, we send forth our prayers and our hopes to those beyond the seas who are maintaining with magnificent valour their battle for freedom. In our unity – our American unity – we will pursue two obvious and simultaneous courses. We will extend to the opponents of force the material resources of this nation, and at the same time will harness and speed up the use of these resources in order that we

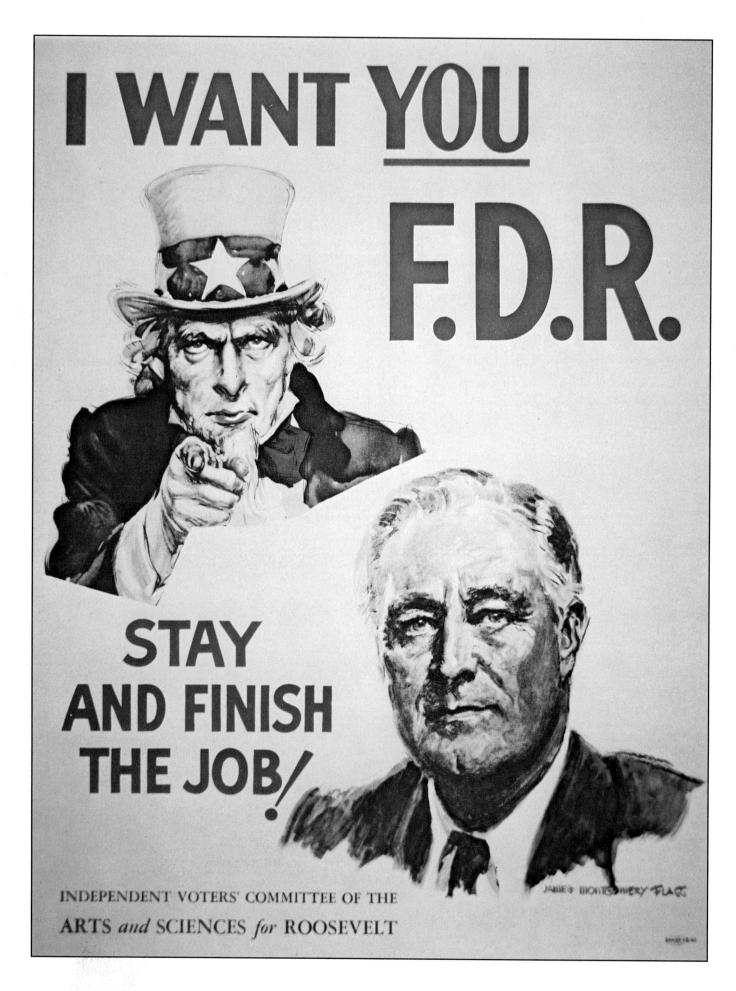

OPPOSITE: FDR was the choice of intellectuals in the 1940 election because of the anti-Nazi foreign policy that was unpopular with the American right.

ABOVE: A campaign button makes a clear statement that overturning the 'no third term' precedent was welcome.

RIGHT: FDR's opponent in the 1940 election was Wendell Willkie, a former Kansas teacher turned Wall Street power company boss whose 'gee whiz' attitude endeared him to an unlikely coalition of isolationists, Nazi sympathisers, Communists, disgruntled Democrats and regular Republicans. But there weren't enough of them to beat the New Deal coalition.

ourselves in the Americas may have equipment and training equal to the task of any emergency and every defence. All roads leading to the accomplishment of these objectives must be kept clear of obstructions. We will not slow down or detour. Signs and signals call for full speed ahead.

There was a pledge that Roosevelt had often given his people, before and after, in speeches across the country: 'I give you one more assurance. I have said this before, but I say it again and again and again – your boys are not going to be sent into any foreign wars.' But now he tempered it with the words: '…except in the case of attack.'

This was now the main plank of his foreign policy; that aggression directly aimed against the United States would be repulsed at all costs. But although most historians concur that he wanted to enter the fight straight away, American public opinion was still against him.

Charles Lindbergh, the great aviator who had been the first to cross the Atlantic in a solo flight, was a thorn in the side of the president. One night the flyer spoke to Americans in a radio broadcast that infuriated FDR. Warning against a war in Europe, he said: 'We [would be forced to] throw the entire resources of our entire nation into the conflict. Munitions alone will not be enough. We are likely to lose a million men, possibly several millions. The best of American youth. We will be staggering under the burden of recovery for the rest of our lives.'

It was a speech that provoked fury in FDR and his response to it highlighted what his critics called his 'Caesar complex'. Congress was bombarded with a million letters praising the Lindbergh speech while polls showed that 80 to 90 per cent of his countrymen agreed with his pacifist views. FDR reacted by starting a whispering campaign that Lindbergh was a Nazi sympathiser, had him removed from the reservist rolls of the air force and ordered his income-tax returns to be audited.

Before fighting the election in November, he transferred to Britain 50 overaged destroyers, destined for the scrapheap, that Churchill desperately needed to keep the submarine-infested sea lanes operating for vital cargo to flow into the beleaguered island nation. In return, FDR received 99-year leases on air and naval

LOOK

ROOSEVELT, CHURCHILL and HITLER
by Dorothy Thompson

1-14-41

NORTH
AMERICA

WHAT WILL HAPPEN TO
CONSCIENTIOUS OBJECTORS?

January 14, 1941 . . .

PRESIDENT ROOSEVELT

SOUTH

LEFT: The Placentia Bay meeting in August 1941 between FDR and Churchill set the tone of Anglo-American wartime co-operation.

bases on Newfoundland, British Guiana, Bermuda and several islands in the West Indies. Churchill needed the ships to maintain the flow of Britain's vital wartime supplies via the convoy system – nearly half of the hundred destroyers available in the Home Fleet had been lost already.

Initially, Roosevelt had hesitated in agreeing this necessary deal with Britain. He had turned down similar requests from France and Norway when the Nazi steamroller had been poised to annihilate them. But he made a bold decision, bypassing Congress entirely to forge the pact leader-to-leader with Churchill. Referring to the acquisition of land in North America from Napoleon, Roosevelt called the deal 'the most important action in the reinforcement of our national defence that has been taken since the Louisiana Purchase'. One effect was certain: it bound the destinies of Britain and the United States together in the dark days that lay ahead.

Japan, which would eventually absorb most of the American war effort, had been cautiously watched by Roosevelt and his advisers as its greed for an Asian empire grew ever more apparent. In July 1940 Roosevelt signed a decree banning the sale of aviation fuel and high-grade steel to Tokyo. In September 1940, when the Japanese signed a treaty alliance with the Axis powers in Europe, the president said: 'There is now only one war. The democracies shall have to unite against a common peril, worldwide in its scope.'

When that war came, FDR would be the man to lead his country in the fight – for on 17 July he entered his third election against Republican Wendell Willkie and won convincingly. Before entering the election, he gave his countrymen a speech which informed them what lay ahead. He told them:

RIGHT: On 31 October 1941 a German submarine torpedoed the destroyer USS *Reuben James*, killing 115 sailors. It was the kind of incident FDR hoped would enrage the wrath of Americans against Germany and for intervening in the European war.

This generation of Americans is living in a tremendous moment of history. The surge of events abroad has made some few doubters among us ask: 'Is this the end of a story that has been told? Is the book of democracy now to be closed away upon the dusty shelves of time?' My answer is this: All we have known of the glories of democracy – its freedom, its efficiency as a mode of living, its ability to meet the aspirations of the common man – all these are merely an introduction to the greater story of a more glorious future. We Americans of today – all of us – are characters in the living book of democracy. But we are also its author. It falls upon us now to say whether the chapters that are to come will tell a story of retreat or a story of continued advance.

His main aim upon being returned to the now-familiar White House was fashioning a policy to contain fascism abroad while his countrymen still yearned for peace. William Leuchtenburg, in his biography *Franklin D Roosevelt and the New Deal*, said: 'He not only announced that half the country's future war production would be allotted to Britain, but in response to an urgent plea from Winston Churchill, unveiled the startling proposal directly to Britain on the understanding that they would be returned or replaced when the war ended.'

LEFT: Charles Lindbergh, the first person to fly the Atlantic solo, ferociously opposed any American intervention in the war. The Lone Eagle became the figurehead leader of the America First movement, on one occasion saying: 'I do not believe we are strong enough to impose our way of life on Europe and on Asia.' FDR, in a vindictive mood, ordered the Internal Revenue Service to subject his tax returns to strict audits and authorised the Department of Justice to place wiretaps on his telephone.

This was the famous Lend-Lease arrangement, formalised the following year, an arrangement which saved Britain from being annihilated for lack of arms, ammunition and supplies. In it, an astonishing $8 billion worth of war materiel was sent across the Atlantic.

In May 1941 the president declared an unlimited state of national emergency, followed by the suspension of all diplomatic relations with the Axis powers in Europe and the freezing of their assets in the United States. In August came the document that formalised the kind of world Roosevelt wanted when the guns had stopped firing. The Atlantic Charter was released after his at-sea meeting with Prime Minister Churchill and pledged the common goal of seeing Nazism defeated, coupled with a lasting peace that would benefit all mankind. Roosevelt still had to tread cautiously with the isolationists, however; there was no mood for war fever and he confided secretly to aides that the nation would need a tremendous jolt for it to be committed to the full-scale horrors of modern combat.

That jolt was about to occur.

ROOSEVELT'S LIEUTENANTS

*Of all the Second World War's national political leaders, only FDR
exercised self-discipline in his interference with military and naval matters.
Largely through good fortune, the United States armed forces had a
competent group of staff officers who emerged just before the war. Three
men provided the professional expertise that guided America's war effort
under Roosevelt's political leadership – although their names may not be
as well known as other more flamboyant military leaders.*

*Ernest J KING (1878-1956), Commander-in-Chief, US Navy
The bad-tempered , self-styled 'sonuvabitch' who was appointed
Commander-in-Chief of the Navy in December 1941 just after the attack
on Pearl Harbor, was renowned in peacetime for his intolerant attitudes,
his hard drinking and his womanising. In his career since graduating from
the US Naval Academy at Annapolis, he had acquired a wide range of
experience in naval affairs, including submarines and naval aviation, the
arms of the service that would dominate the war at sea.*

*King had learned his trade at a time when the work of the great
American naval historian, Alfred Thayer Mahan, dominated Navy
thinking. According to Mahan, the admiral's plan of action had to be an
aggressive one, to seek out the decisive battle with the enemy's main fleet
and destroy as many of the enemy's ships with little regard to one's own
losses. And so, when King drew up a strategy for the US Navy in early
1942 he emphasised a threefold approach: support the British war effort in
North Africa, defend the sea lanes to ensure Great Britain would remain
as a base for the eventual invasion of Europe and attack the Japanese
where ever possible. The last of these aims struck many at the highest
levels of the American war effort as rash beyond belief.*

*King's vision of the war proved remarkably accurate when he deployed
it to gain more resources for the war against Japan at the Casablanca
conference in February 1943. He believed that the Soviet Union 'will do
nine-tenths of the job of defeating Germany.' He argued against an
invasion of Italy as a diversion from the main effort, but for an invasion
of northern France as soon as possible. And – uniquely at the time – he
considered the United States had sufficient industrial power to supply the
munitions for offensives in both Europe and the Pacific.*

*George C MARSHALL (1880-1959), Chief of Staff, US Army
By a coincidence, Marshall took his oath of office the day German forces
attacked Poland. His most outstanding characteristic was a willingness to
express his disagreement with superiors in a polite yet firm manner.
Marshall's most influential impact on the war occurred before it had even
started. He created the conditions that allowed the rapid expansion of the*

US Army once war broke out, partly by getting conscription introduced in 1940, and partly by developing a method for creating new divisions quickly from a cadre of serving officers and men. The training system ensured those inducted into the army would learn the craft of soldiering thoroughly.

During the war Marshall pressed adamantly for an invasion of northern France as soon as possible, preferably in the autumn of 1942. But while in the years between 1939 and 1941 he achieved many goals, this one was denied him. Instead, in November 1942 combined British and American forces invaded North Africa with the effect of postponing the eventual Operation Overlord until 1944. It was the greatest setback of his career.

After the war he became secretary of state and sponsored the European Recovery Program, or Marshall Plan, which poured huge sums of American money into war-devastated Europe in an attempt to forestall the rise of left-wing political forces. The plan was a huge success, and established close American involvement in European affairs for some 40 years. Marshall won the Nobel Peace Prize in 1953.

LEFT: 'Hap' Arnold commanded the United States Army Air Force during the war. Arnold was a skilled proponent of the potential of air power in the next war at a time of grave scepticism in the interwar army.

Henry H ARNOLD (1886-1950), chief of the Air Corps
Before the Second World War, anyone who suggested that aeroplanes
would change the nature of warfare had to be very determined to press
this point of view in a military world dominated by those who were
unlikely to have had any experience of flight. Fortunately for the US
Army Air Force, Arnold was just the sort of visionary to make a relentless
pursuit of the airpower goal.

Arnold had learned to fly in 1911, as a young second lieutenant
attached to the Signal Corps. Like most early aviators, he understood
exactly how flying machines worked, learning how to take one apart and
put it back together. He never saw combat during the First World War
because, as one of the few air officers in the Army, he was assistant
director of military aeronautics.

Arnold's view of air warfare took as its model the concept of an
independent air force as existed in the shape of Britain's Royal Air Force.
The RAF believed that its main mission was to bomb enemy factories and
destroy the means by which the war effort was carried on. The doctrine of

strategic bombing was similiarly accepted by the USAAF, only to be proved wanting in the skies over Europe. Bombers were incapable of delivering the knockout blow to enemy industry on their own.

In spite of this, Arnold still allowed the demand s of a strategic bombing campaign to determine his outlook on the major military disputes of the time. His influence in the American war effort was in directing the Army or the Navy towards operations that would allow USAAF bombers to hit Germany or Japan.

ABOVE: The theatrical Douglas MacArthur returns to the Philippines on 21 October 1944. He commanded the South-West Pacific theatre in the war.

OPPOSITE PAGE:
TOP LEFT: Chester Nimitz commanded the Pacific Fleet during the war, and also the Central Pacific theatre.

TOP RIGHT: Admiral William F Halsey USN. His carriers were absent from Pearl Harbor on the 'Day of Infamy'.

RIGHT: Dwight D Eisenhower was appointed Supreme Commander in Europe.

A STATE OF WAR

IN the end, it was the lust of the empire of Japan, not the avarice of Hitler, that provided the impetus for the United States to go to war. On the morning of 7 December 1941, Japanese carrier-based planes attacked the naval base at Pearl Harbor in Hawaii, the home port of the mighty Pacific Fleet.

Guam, the Philippines, Midway Island, Hong Kong and the Malay peninsula were also attacked. But by far the greatest damage was sustained in the supposedly safe waters of Pearl Harbor. Because it was a Sunday, most American warships were docked or at anchor in the shallows. The Japanese planes sunk or disabled 19 vessels, including eight battleships and three destroyers. More than 140 aircraft were destroyed and 2300 people, mostly sailors and soldiers, were killed.

President Roosevelt, who had had to wrestle with the problems of bringing into a war a nation made up of immigrants – of Germans, Italians, Asians and numerous other nationalities – now found a sense of national unity that previous leaders seeking for a consensus would have envied. He stayed late in the Oval Office that night, preparing a speech that would signal the beginning of the Allied whirlwind.

Roosevelt addressed Congress the next day, bringing the United States into a war for which civilised conduct among men and nations was ultimately at stake. He spoke in slow, solemn tones in a speech that has gone down in history. He told the assembled representatives:

Yesterday, December 7th, 1941 – a date which will live in infamy – the United States of America was suddenly and deliberately attacked by naval and air forces of the empire of Japan... The attack yesterday on the Hawaiian islands has caused severe damage to American naval and military forces. Very many

ABOVE: US troops defend a Hawaiian airfield in December 1941. The Japanese were surprised by the US forces lack of preparedness at a time of international crisis.

RIGHT: FDR signs the declaration of war against Japan passed by Congress on 8 December 1941.

OPPOSITE: Battleship Row at Pearl Harbor burns on 7 December 1941 during the Japanese attack.

LEFT: The USS Yorktown sinking after being badly damaged by Japanese aircraft during the battle of Midway on 4 June 1942.

OPPOSITE: Ensign George Gay, the only survivor of Torpedo Eight's gallant but doomed attack on the Japanese aircraft carrier *Kaga*, is comforted by a nurse as he reads about the battle.

American lives have been lost. In addition, American ships have been reported torpedoed on the high seas between San Francisco and Honolulu... I have directed that all measures be taken for our defence. Always will we remember the character of the onslaught against us. No matter how long it may take us to overcome this premeditated invasion, the American people, in their righteous might, will win through to absolute victory. I believe I interpret the will of the Congress and of the people when I assert that we will not only defend ourselves to the uttermost, but will make very certain that this form of treachery shall never endanger us again. Hostilities exist; there is no blinking at the fact that our people, our territory and our interests are in grave danger. With confidence in our armed forces, with the unbounded determination of our people, we will gain the inevitable triumph, so help us God. I ask that the Congress declare that since the unprovoked and dastardly attack by Japan on Sunday December 7, a state of war has existed between the United States and the Japanese empire.

Mobilising the resources of the greatest industrial power on earth was a complex task but one which Roosevelt was more than up to. His health was in decline now, although he never admitted it, least of all to the White House physician who covered up the knowledge of his weakened arteries and strained heart due to heavy smoking. Yet his mind was, like the ageing Churchill's, honed to the task of smashing the Axis foes in every theatre of war.

The newly created US War Production Board was given the task of maximising production in every single factory, filling the ranks of workers who went off to war with children and women in their place. When Roosevelt became president in the 1930s, his nation had 20 per cent unemployment. By the time his 'arsenal of democracy' was firing at full pitch, there was only just over one per cent of people actually looking for a job. By the time 1942 dawned, Roosevelt knew that, with the industrial might of North America, victory was only a matter of time.

Roosevelt was the only leader of the wartime Big Three – the others being Stalin and Churchill – whose choice of commanders was almost perfect from the outset. Whereas Churchill dismissed generals willy-nilly before the decisive desert victory of El Alamein, and Stalin shot commanders who failed in the field, Roosevelt found in Nimitz, Marshall and mainly in Dwight David Eisenhower, men he could work with. In his book on the Second World War mentioned earlier, Robert Leckie wrote: 'It is doubtful if Franklin

Delano Roosevelt ever made a better appointment than to name Dwight David Eisenhower to the most coveted command in the history of warfare.'

Roosevelt – with Europe besieged, the Soviet Union at the point of total collapse and the Orient overrun by the Japanese – found himself not just the leader of the United States, but the leader of the Free World. However, the pressures of office weighed heavily on him during his third term. His health was failing gradually – largely a result of heavy smoking – and he pushed himself harder and harder. His days still began before 9 a.m. with breakfast in bed, surrounded by newspapers from all over the United States. His executive business, including appointments, briefings and meetings, stretched from 10 a.m. until beyond 6 p.m., with lunch usually eaten on a tray in the middle of a meeting. Then he would have a short nap before continuing work until late in the evening.

Apart from the conduct of the war, which he wanted won in the shortest possible time with the minimum number of American casualties, Roosevelt's burning passion was for the success of a world organisation for peace, a successful League of Nations that would bind all countries together in harmony. This organisation was called the United Nations. The cynical Stalin would pay lip service to it and Churchill would fret that the 'fumbling fingers of 40 or 50 nations' would only serve to assist in the break-up of the British Empire – but Roosevelt cherished its ideals with the love of the zealot.

In his speech to the new Congress on 7 January 1943, his usual formidable majority having been wiped out by a Republican surge in the polls, Roosevelt outlined his vision for a world after victory:

Victory in this war is the first and greatest goal before us. Victory in the peace is the next. That means striving toward the enlargement of the security of man here and throughout the world and, finally, striving for the Fourth Freedom: Freedom from Fear. It is of little account for any of us to talk of essential human needs, of attaining security, if we run the risk of another world war in 10 or 20 or 50 years. That is just plain common sense… I shudder to think of what will happen to humanity, including ourselves, if this war ends in an inconclusive peace and another war breaks out when the babies of today have grown to fighting age.

LEFT: Casablanca, 24 January 1943. From left to right: General Giraud, FDR, General de Gaulle and Winston Churchill.

OPPOSITE: Quebec, August 1943. From left to right: seated, Mackenzie King, Canadian Premier, FDR, Churchill; standing, Brooke, King, Dill, Marshall.

LEFT: War in the Pacific: US Marines in combat on Tarawa, 20 November 1943.

OPPOSITE: War in Europe: D-Day plus 2, 8 June 1944. 2nd US Infantry Division marches inland from Omaha Beach.

Conferences in these middle war years were held to formulate the postwar world, beginning with a summit between Roosevelt and Churchill in Casablanca in January 1943. Stalin had intended to be present but in the event the decisive battle of the war against Germany, at Stalingrad, was under way at the time, and he remained at his post in the Kremlin.

It was at Casablanca that Roosevelt announced the Allied policy of demanding no less than unconditional surrender from the Axis powers. There was to be no negotiated peace, no chance of anything other than the total subjugation of the enemy. His critics later said he lost many hundreds of thousands of Allied lives with this declaration, giving the Germans in particular added steel to 'fight to the finish' as they had nothing left to lose. But Roosevelt was adamant; in the new world he envisioned, there was no room for backroom deals and secret covenants. He spoke his mind and he stood by it.

Summits followed at Quebec, Cairo and Tehran, the first two attended by Roosevelt and Churchill and their attendant warlords, the last with Stalin present. On the agenda were China, the war in the Far East, the Free French, collaboration on atomic energy and the Balkans. But it was at Tehran, staged at the end of November 1943, that Stalin began his manipulations to create a Soviet empire that would stretch across

US forces fought their way from the beaches of Normandy to the heart of the Third Reich's homeland. The photographs on these pages give a graphic impression of the bitterness of the fighting.

LEFT: **Fighting on Guam, July 1944. It was action like this which would lead the US to drop the atomic bomb to save American troops' lives.**

Europe when the guns finally fell silent. Roosevelt outlined a plan to the wily Soviet dictator for 'Four Policemen' – the United States, Britain, the USSR and China – to help ensure world stability. It was a plan scorned by Stalin, however, who was already scheming to install a pro-Soviet regime in Poland.

FDR thought he could read Stalin well, but in this he was grossly mistaken. As FDR forged ahead with his plan for a United Nations, Stalin was intent on taking what he wanted as the spoils of war, and to hell with anyone who disagreed with him. The only positive things to emerge from the conference were the agreement for Britain and the US to launch the invasion of France the following year and for the Soviet Union to enter the war again Japan at some date in the future.

Humanitarianism and striving for the establishment of the United Nations were FDR's genuine aims as the war progressed. So it was a surprising departure, therefore, in September 1944, long after the Allied armies had landed in Normandy and were on the path to victory, that he advocated a plan which would have meant incredible hardship to the surviving German people had it been implemented. Roosevelt stood by the Morgenthau Plan, formulated by his treasury secretary, to strip Germany of all her heavy industries and to turn her people back into peasants in an agricultural nation.

LEFT: One of FDR's broadcasting favourites: Walter Winchell regularly spoke out for Roosevelt.

OPPOSITE: All quiet on the home front? The Republicans made an issue of Roosevelt's son's rank in this songsheet.

Roosevelt's endorsement of this policy – seen by Churchill, his own secretary of war and the general public as nothing less than supervised starvation and subjugation of the Germans – caused a huge outcry in the United States. Some historians think he was merely trying to prove to Stalin that he could be as forceful as the Soviets (although he had opposed an earlier proposal from the dictator that 50,000 German officers should be shot out of hand).

In the end, however, his own cabinet forced him to reconsider and the Morgenthau Plan was quietly shelved in favour of occupation zones that would be administered by the four powers: the United States, the USSR, France and Great Britain. In these zones, de-Nazification, and not wholesale vengeance on the German people, would be the main task.

THE LOST GOALS

IN November 1944 Roosevelt pulled off what has never been matched before or since – a fourth term of office as president of the United States. On a cold 7 November day he was elected with yet another convincing majority, many of the ballots coming in from serving front-line troops in all the theatres of the war he was committed to winning. Yet his health seemed to suffer in direct contrast to the progress made by the armies at the front.

Shortly before the election, Robert Sherwood, who was to become his chief speech writer, described him thus: 'I had not seen the president for eight months and I was shocked by his appearance. I had heard that he had lost a lot of weight but I was unprepared for the almost ravaged appearance of his face. He had his coat off and his shirt collar seemed several sizes too large for his emaciated neck. Yet he also seemed to be more full of good humour and fight than ever.'

Roosevelt's appeal to the common man is illustrated at this time with a speech he gave to the Teamsters, the powerful labour union that controlled distribution and so kept the machinery of war oiled and moving. FDR had come under yet more blistering attacks from Republican rivals, claiming he was again moving the country towards dictatorship. They also attacked his wife and his sons – vicious, personal attacks that seemed out of step with the times. Roosevelt used his keen sense of humour – and his dog – to deflate them. In his speech, he told the union men:

> The Republican leaders have not been content to make personal attacks on me or my wife or my sons; they now include my little dog Fala. Unlike the members of my family, Fala resents this. When he learned that the Republican fiction writers had concocted a story that I had left him behind on an Aleutian Island and had sent a destroyer back to find him – at a cost to the taxpayer of 2 or 3 or 20

LEFT: **Roosevelt campaigners in 1944 – an unprecedented fourth term as president followed.**

RIGHT: The losing Republican presidential candidate in 1944 was Thomas E Dewey.

RIGHT: *The New York Times* heralds FDR's victory.

LEFT: FDR and vice-president elect Harry S Truman after the 1944 election victory.

OPPOSITE: FDR gives his inaugural address from the White House, January 1945.

million dollars – his Scotch soul was furious. He has not been the same dog since. I am accustomed to hearing malicious falsehoods about myself, but I think I have a right to object to libelous statements about my dog!

It was also at this time, and certainly no laughing matter for Eleanor, that Roosevelt's affair with Lucy Mercer was rekindled upon the death of her husband.

Early in 1945 Roosevelt embarked on what he sincerely hoped would be his biggest foreign policy success of the war. Tragically, it was one which turned into the biggest disaster for him, Churchill and much of the free world. In February, just months before the end of the war in all theatres of operations, the Big Three – the United States, Britain and the Soviet Union – convened a conference at Yalta, in the Crimea, for a pow-wow that would settle the fate of nations.

It was at Yalta that Roosevelt finally and fully misplaced his faith in Stalin's word, convinced against all available evidence that the Soviet dictator was motivated by the same aims and emotions as he and was equally moving towards the same goals in Europe that he cherished: freedom for all, an end to colonialism and the right of peoples in occupied lands to choose their own destinies. Stalin, of course, wanted none of this. He planned to become the biggest coloniser of them all, extending a sphere of influence from the Kremlin that would stretch across Europe to Berlin and from the Baltic to the Mediterranean.

'The colonial system means war,' Roosevelt had said to his son, Elliott, before attending the conference. 'I will have none of it.' But it was the wily Stalin who won out at Yalta. He was the smiling bear and Roosevelt his trusting victim. It was only later realised just how far Roosevelt had gone in signing away nations to decades of oppression under the Communist yoke. In postwar years, the president's kindest critics attributed his misplaced trust and his ill-advised surrenders at Yalta to the fact that Roosevelt was a dying man.

Perhaps FDR's greatest single mistake was in agreeing to the veto power of the USSR in the UN Security Council, in which the Soviets would become one of the five powers on the council with the power to bow

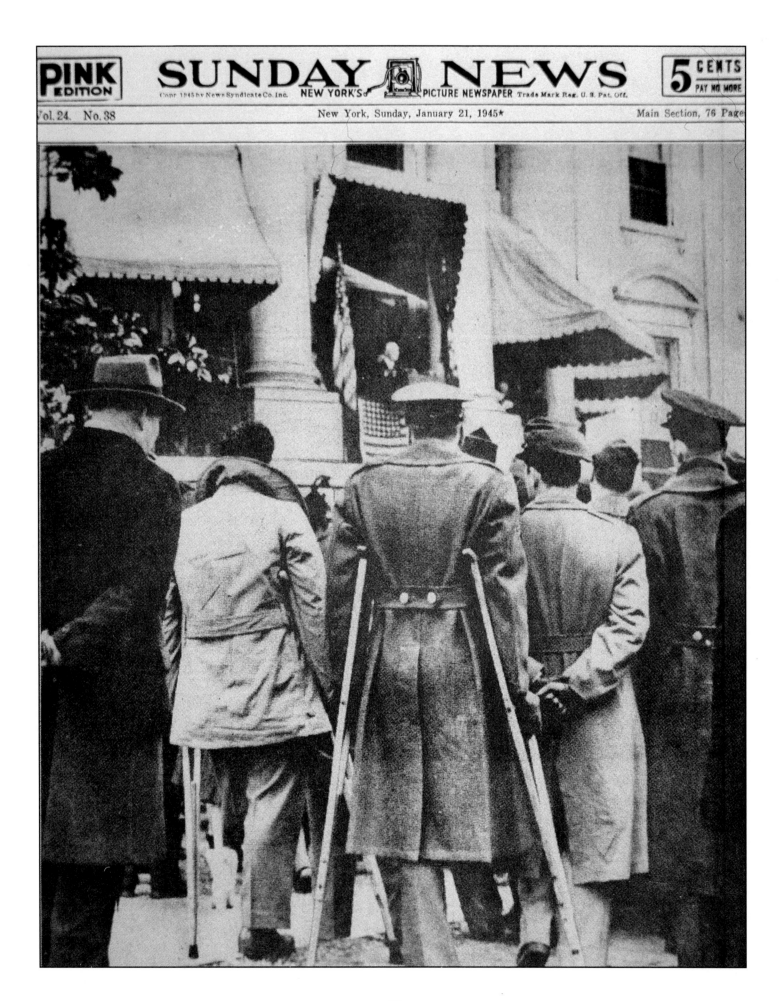

out of international rules whenever it pleased. This was a veto that would be used often in the peacetime world.

Roosevelt and Churchill also vacillated on Poland – the country for which Britain had gone to war in the first place. Now the Western allies gave Stalin a clear field to make it one of his empire's largest satellite states.

Likewise, the president was so eager for Stalin to turn his formidable Red Army against Japan that he made another overgenerous concession. He did nothing when the great dictator announced that he would be seizing the Kurile Islands from Japan and sought the old tsarist privileges along the Chinese Eastern Railway and to control the ports of Port Arthur and Darien (now Lüda). This was a direct break of the promise that Roosevelt had made to Chinese nationalist leader Chiang Kai-Shek in 1943. At that time, the president had pledged that Chinese land was sacrosanct and that the United States would prevent any return to the sort of colonialism China had suffered at the turn of the century.

Roosevelt and his staff had a childlike, naive faith in Stalin's intentions, seemingly failing to grasp the realities of the Soviet leaders designs. Edward Stettinius, his secretary of state, said: 'There was immense pressure put on our president by our military leaders to bring the USSR into the war against Japan. At this time the atomic bomb was still an unknown quantity and our setback in the Battle of the Bulge was fresh in the minds of everybody. We had not yet crossed the Rhine. No one knew how long the European war would last nor how great the casualties would be.'

ABOVE: US Marines raise the flag over Iwo Jima in Joe Rosenthal's classic photograph.

RIGHT: Yalta, 9 February 1945: the dying Roosevelt embarks on what he hoped would be his biggest foreign policy success of the war. Tragically, it would turn into a disaster for much of the free world.

OPPOSITE: Eleanor and 13 grandchildren celebrate with FDR on his fourth inauguration day.

Some of Roosevelt's top commanders in the field had his ear and told him that it might cost one million more American deaths to subdue the despots in Tokyo. At Yalta, Roosevelt gave way to Stalin in the genuine belief that Soviet intervention in the war in the Far East would save American boys' lives. Stalin made many promises at Yalta but kept none of them – and the West could later only sit back and watch as his Iron Curtain was drawn across Europe.

In *Europe in Our Time*, by Walter Laquer, Roosevelt at Yalta is portrayed as a man out of his depth with the realpolitik of the age. He wrote:

Roosevelt had a superb feeling for domestic politics; his experience in foreign affairs was more limited. In his dealings he revealed a mixture of cleverness and naivety, and even in retrospect it is not easy to establish where one began and the other ended. He hoped that co-operation with the Soviet Union would continue after the war; he had a hunch, he said, that Stalin would co-operate. He dealt with him, and the Soviet Union in general, as he would have treated a dissenting faction within the Democratic Party, hoping that from the usual give-and-take that constitutes American politics consensus would emerge.

Yet, in Stalin, FDR was dealing with a dictator whose crimes against his own people sometimes made Hitler look like a mere apprentice in the black arts of murder and torture.

LEFT: Churchill and Roosevelt vacillated over Poland – the country for which Britain had gone to war – and Stalin was able to make it one of his empire's largest satellite states. Churchill is seen here at Chartwell, postwar, with Bernard M Baruch who in 1946 presented the US plan for atomic energy control to the UN.

OPPOSITE: Harry Hopkins was used by FDR as a special envoy to the UK during the war establishing a close working relationship with Churchill – he was dubbed 'Roosevelt's own foreign office'.

BOWED HEARTS

ROOSEVELT, always careless about his health and scornful of the doctors whose duty it was to care for him, took a train in April 1945 to the Little White House in Warm Springs to recover from a persistent sinus infection. Mrs Roosevelt did not accompany him. Aboard his personal train with him was his mistress Lucy Mercer, two female cousins and some staff members.

On 12 April the president was sitting for a portrait by the water-colour artist Elizabeth Shoumatoff, who had done earlier paintings of him. He broke for lunch shortly after 1 p.m., telling his cousin Margaret Suckley: 'I have a terrific headache.'

He died at 3.35 p.m. that same day from a massive cerebral haemorrhage brought on by chronic arteriosclerosis. He was 63 years old. His death came less than one month before the surrender of Nazi Germany, and less than four months before the crushing of Japan.

Congress and the nation were stunned by his sudden passing. People felt a great void had suddenly opened up in national life. Senator Arthur Vandenberg spoke to an eerily silent Senate in praise of the great man:

In this hour of anxious tragedy, when the bowed hearts of all the civilised earth join ours this fateful morning in humble, poignant sorrow that Franklin Delano Roosevelt, the 31st president of the United States, has been gathered to his fathers, nothing that we can say here can add to the glory of his stature or the measure of our grief.

LEFT: A nation mourns...

OPPOSITE: ... but the war continues. Rocket ships bombard Okinawa.

He belongs now to history, where he leaves a mark which not even rushing centuries can erase. Those who were his loyal opposition, no less than those who were his intimate associates, have always recognised in him a rare crusader for his human faiths and amazing genius on behalf of his always vigorous ideals, a valiant knight in the armour of his commandership as he waged global war.

He bravely mastered his own physical handicap with a courage which never lapsed as he fought his way to an unprecedented pinnacle at home and to dominant influence around the world. His untimely death will be mourned at every hearthstone and on every battlefront where freedom wins the victory to which he literally gave his life. A successful peace must be his monument.

So ended the life of one of the greatest statesmen the world had ever seen. As we now know, instead of the permanent peace he had dreamed of, a fragile one came to pass, pockmarked with all man's usual petty vanities and jealousies that flare into bloody warfare. Nevertheless, Roosevelt's UN vision became a reality and many times since the end of the Second World War, the organisation he battled to make a reality has eased suffering, averted global conflicts and aided millions of refugees.

Flawed as any other human – unfaithful, sometimes venal, selfish and autocratic – FDR was undoubtedly endowed with qualities which made him the natural defender of the free world in the face of unrivalled tyranny. *Webster's American Biographies* said of him:

STRENGTH TO YOUR ARM, MR. PRESIDENT

LEFT: Cartoon comment by Fitzpatrick in the *St Louis Post-Dispatch*, 15 April 1945.

OPPOSITE: FDR's funeral cortège, Washington 1945.

Roosevelt was probably the most ardently admired, even loved, and the most heartily hated and feared president in American history. Evaluations of his role range from saviour of the nation to would-be dictator. Doubtless his administration was highly effective in many ways, and he provided a style of leadership seldom matched. A skilled politician, an engaging campaigner, a bold and pragmatic president and a far-sighted world leader, he left a permanent mark on the nation and the world.

Franklin Roosevelt had himself penned a speech which he intended to deliver before Congress the following week. Although he was never able to voice it, it stands the test of time as the most fitting eulogy of the man. He wrote: 'Today we are faced with the pre-eminent fact that, if civilisation is to survive, we must cultivate the science of human relationships – the ability of all peoples, of all kinds, to live together and to work together in the same world. At peace.'

LEFT: Franklin Delano Roosevelt, 1882-1945.

BELOW: In the depths of the Great Depression, signing the unemployment relief bill, 1933.

OPPOSITE: A skilled politician, an engaging campaigner, a bold and pragmatic president.

PRINCIPAL DATES

1882   Born Hyde Park, New York, on 30 January.

1904   Bachelor of Arts Degree in Law, Harvard University.

1905   Married to Eleanor Roosevelt.

1910   First political victory, elected to state Senate on Democratic ticket.

1912   Re-elected to Senate after campaigning successfully for Woodrow Wilson.

1913   President Wilson rewards Roosevelt with job of Assistant Secretary, Navy.

1921   Stricken with polio, effectively paralysing him below waist level.

1924   Attends Democrat National Convention after convalescence.

1928   Elected Governor of New York.

1930   Wins re-election for Governor due to success of reforms aimed at easing
suffering of working man.

1932   Wins Democratic nomination for the presidency, and easily defeats
incumbent Herbert Hoover in November.

1933   Inaugurated president on 4 March.

1935   Supreme Court invalidates several New Deal laws.

1936   Roosevelt wins landslide re-election.

1937   Attempts to 'pack' Supreme Court with liberal judges, causing firestorm
of criticism that he is edging close to dictatorship.

1938   Sides with free European nations against Hitler and Mussolini while
avowing strong isolationist policies to keep the United States out of the war.

1939   Plays host in Washington to British monarchy. Privately acknowledges
that the United States will probably have to go to war against tyrants in Europe
and the Far East.

1940   Trades old naval destroyers with Britain in return for strategic bases
on British Empire lands.
Wins third term of office.

1941   Vows 'all aid short of war' to Allies. Brings the United States into war after
Japanese attack Pacific Fleet in Pearl Harbor on 7 December.

1943   The conferences of Casablanca, Quebec and Tehran in which Roosevelt
sketches out his vision of the UN and a peaceful postwar world.

1944   Unprecedented fourth term of office. Health poor due to arteriosclerosis.

1945   Yalta Conference. Churchill and Roosevelt duped by Stalin, paving way
for Cold War.

1945   His death on 12 April followed by state funeral with full honours.